THIS IS GOD'S WORLD

By Dean Walley
Illustrated by
Frances Yamashita

♛ HALLMARK
CROWN EDITIONS

This is God's world....

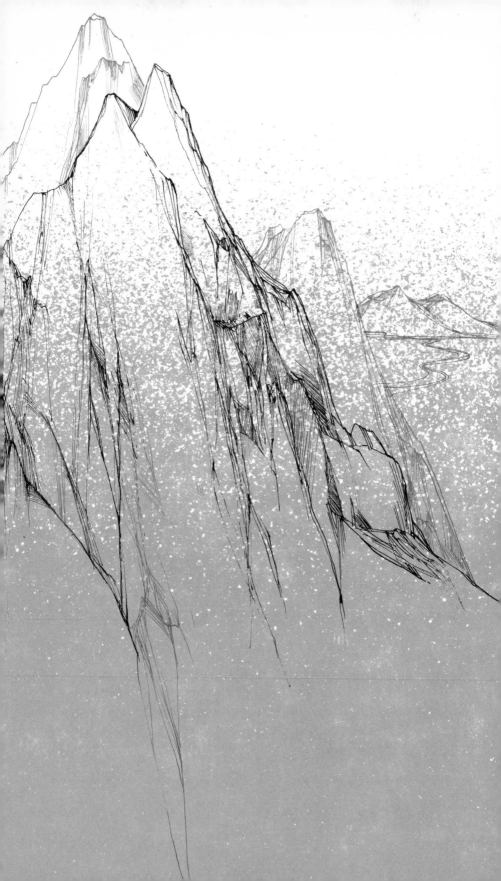

We see His signature on all creations....

His name of power

crowns the mountain peaks....

....and swirls across the seas....

His name of wonder

is etched on every perfect snowflake....

....and is silhouetted by the triumph

of each sunrise....

And in the faces of His silent creatures

who live in the forests....

He has written His name of love....

Every flower is a beautiful sign to us....

that our world is God's world.

For they toil not

....neither do they spin....

yet God has stooped from heaven

to fashion their fragile blossoms....

He has blessed the earth

with the rainbow luxury of flowers....

to lift up our hearts....

By the fullness of heaven and earth,

we know God.

Who else but God....in His infinite wisdom....

would stretch rivers like silver ribbons

across the continents....

....or gently lay green blankets across the rolling hills....

....or fill the darkest recesses of the oceans

with life?

Only God could conceive

    the enormous sundowns

that vault the horizon

    in awesome majesty....

Only God could pierce the sky with stars....

that we might look into His heaven.

And the world God has made is a holy place....

It is His own cathedral....

    filled with birds singing anthems of praise....

    ....graced with the ritual of the changing seasons....

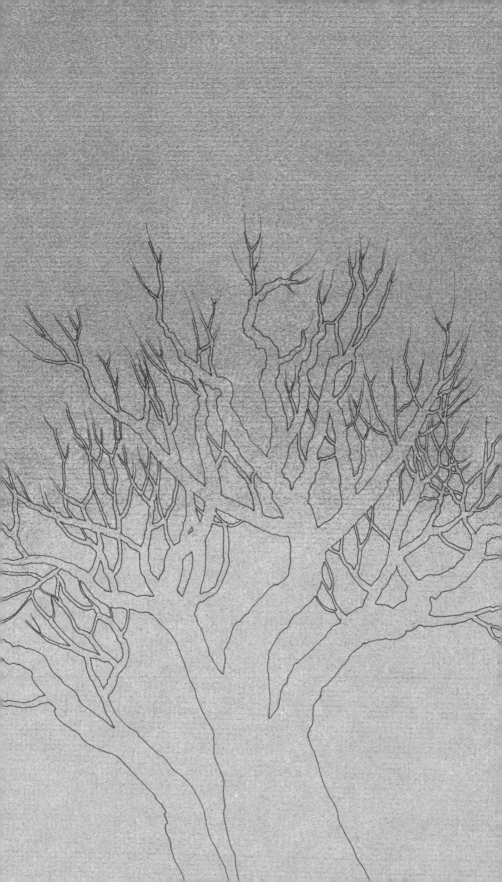

It is a place of reverence....

    where man can worship freely under the blue dome

    of the sky....

    ....and join the host of living things

        that reach for God....

God's world is full of knowledge and inspiration.

....we can find sermons in stone....

....there are pathways to follow that lead

away from self....and close to the heart of God....

The wild beasts can teach us nobility and courage....

....we can learn humility from the violet....

.... and steadfastness from a star....

And our hearts are filled with joy....when we realize
that we not only live in this world God has made
....but that we are part of His creation.
And as He cares for all His own
....He cares for us.

As He directs the flight of the smallest swallow

....He will direct our path

....and even in the shadowed valleys

we need fear no evil....

As He arranges the silent stars in harmony and beauty....

    so can He arrange the pattern

        of our lives....helping us create order....

            giving us an inner harmony

            that makes us whole....

....As He loves all of His creations

....so will He love us

....throughout eternity....

Yes, this is God's world....

a world that He has fashioned for us....

....and just as the moon reflects the brilliance
and splendor of the sun....

....so can our lives reflect the power and glory....

....the joy and beauty....

....of God, in whose image we are created....

This book was designed and illustrated by Frances Yamashita.
The artist made her own color separations
and closely supervised the printing for utmost accuracy
of reproduction. The type is set in Optima, a roman face
of graceful simplicity designed by Hermann Zapf.
The paper is Hallclear, White Imitation Parchment and Ivory
Fiesta Parchment. The cover is bound with imported
natural Seta silk book cloth and Torino paper.